LUTHER *on* LEADERSHIP

Life-Changing Classics, Vol. XXI

LUTHER *on* LEADERSHIP

Stephen J. Nichols
President of Reformation Bible College
Sanford, Florida

TREMENDOUS LEADERSHIP
Leadership with a kick!

Life-Changing Classics, Vol. XXI

LUTHER *on* LEADERSHIP

Published by:
Tremendous Leadership
PO Box 267
Boiling Springs, PA 17007
717-701-8159

www.TremendousLeadership.com

ISBN: 978-1-936354-55-9

Cover Design: Karen Webb

First Edition

Printed in the United States of America

Table of Contents

Foreword

One of the many attributes I appreciate about Dr. Tracey Jones is her ability to extract leadership lessons from virtually any setting. Just as remarkable is her ability to identify leader scholars such as Dr. Stephen J. Nichols, the president of Reformation Bible College in Sanford, Florida. In his signature style of acumen, balanced with real-world application, Dr. Nichols leads us through a study of the exceptional life and ministry of an obscure theologian who changed the face of Christianity for centuries to come. I know that voice well as Dr. Nichols and I shared the privilege of serving together at Lancaster

Bible College, Lancaster, Pennsylvania, for sixteen years.

Dr. Nichols walks us through the medical, cultural, economic, and spiritual darkness of the days in which Luther lived and the faith that shaped this sixteenth-century monk's perspectives. He introduces us to the concept of *battle communication*—its clarion call and the very nature of its transcendent answer. Dr. Nichols guides us into the deep struggle of *anfechtungen*, which shaped Luther through strife so that he delivered the famous declaration, "Here I stand. I can do no other."—thus displaying Luther's servant leadership for all to see. Finally, he engages us with the secret to generational influence.

I am confident that you and your leadership will be challenged and strengthened by these lessons, highlighted as only Dr. Nichols can. From his own deep well of humility, he stirs our souls to resonate with Luther's final words, "We are beggars. This is true." Reading these pages is like sharing a cup of coffee with my friend and colleague. How appropriate we sample these leadership lessons from Martin Luther as the world celebrates the 500th anniversary of the Reformation in October 2017.

Dr. Peter W. Teague, President
Lancaster Bible College |
Capital Seminary & Graduate School

Introduction

Peter Drucker famously quipped, "The only definition of a leader is someone who has followers." By that definition, Martin Luther is one of the greatest leaders this world has ever seen. There are an estimated 800 to 900 million Protestants worldwide today. All Protestants trace their roots back to Martin Luther and to one day in the sixteenth century—October 31, 1517.

In Luther's day October 31st was celebrated as "All Hallow's Eve." It marked the night before "All Saints' Day," celebrated on November 1st. As "All Saints' Day" approached in 1517, a monk sat in his study in the university town of Wittenberg, about sixty-five miles away from Berlin. He was troubled by the abuses and excesses of his church. Manipulative practices and fraud ran deep as people were exploited. They were being conned into believing that they could buy their way into heaven. This troubled that monk, who was unknown and obscure at the time. He was not highly positioned, and he had no platform, yet he was committed to the truth. That monk was Martin Luther.

Martin Luther had been trained as a scholar, so he plied the tools of his trade—his desk, his pen and inkwell, and paper. With great conviction of heart that day in his university study, he sat down to write about the injustices and untruths he observed. The result was a list of ninety-five theses that he wanted to debate with his church. When he completed the list, he grabbed a mallet and a nail and carried the list to Castle Church in Wittenberg where he hammered it on the church door. His life, the church, his nation, and even the entire world would never be the same. The posting of "The Ninety-Five Theses" was only the beginning. Martin Luther would live and struggle and contend for the truth over the next decades until his death on February 18, 1546.

Luther lived a truly larger-than-life existence, as evidenced by his stunning leadership of a church and university in Wittenberg. His ideas and influence soon spread across German lands, then across the whole of Europe, and eventually to the four corners of the earth.

Luther is often celebrated as an historical figure, a pastor, and a fiery Reformer, but he was also a leader. Fully 500 years after his bold move at the door of the church in Wittenberg, we continue to discuss and even celebrate Luther and his achievement. That is the legacy of a true leader.

Luther offered five essential lessons for leaders. Each lesson was colorfully displayed in his life.

Leadership Lesson #1:
The most timely message
is timeless truth.

Leadership Lesson #2:
Boldness and confidence come not
from within, but from God.

Leadership Lesson #3:
All leaders will face opposition, conflict,
distortion, rejection, suffering, and loss—
and know how to persevere through all of it.

Leadership Lesson #4:
Never underestimate the
potential of children.

Leadership Lesson #5:
Leaders serve.

Let's step into Dr. Luther's classroom and explore each of these five lessons.

LEADERSHIP LESSON #1

Timeless Truth

The most timely message
is timeless truth.

The situation could not have been more dire in the sixteenth century. Of course, they didn't have bumper stickers in the Middle Ages, but if they did, one of them would have read: "In the Midst of Life, We Die ."

The plague washed over Europe in waves from the time of the fourteenth century onwards. The Black Plague, or Black Death, ravaged Europe, taking at least one third of its population. Imagine if every third family on your street were just gone within the space of a few months. Imagine if one third of your coworkers just vanished. After the great plague swept through, many small scale plagues wreaked havoc for the next several centuries. Even Luther's Wittenberg faced two such plagues in the 1520s. The time of Martin Luther was a time of death.

The time of Martin Luther was also a time of darkness. Few people could read. Less than one percent of the population was literate. Even most of the priests were uneducated and illiterate. They mumbled through the mass, and the congregation didn't know any better. It was a time of intellectual darkness.

The days in which Martin Luther lived were also characterized by economic darkness. Society was composed of essentially four classes: the nobles, knights, priests (as well as monks and nuns), and peasants, but the vast majority of people were in the peasant class. Most peasants scratched out a subsistence living. This was not a meritocracy. You could have all the talent and skill in the world, but, with few exceptions, you were class-bound. In addition to intellectual and economic darkness, Luther lived in a time of cultural darkness. The explosion of the arts in the time of the Renaissance was far off on the horizon. Great cathedrals, breathtaking in their grandeur and beauty, were scattered across Europe. Art continued to be produced, but for most towns and cities and for most of the people in the Middle Ages, the arts eluded their grasp.

Luther's world was also a time of spiritual darkness. According to the apostle Paul, we are born dead in our trespasses and sins. According to the Apostle John, we are born in darkness. Death and darkness. In His grace and mercy, God has provided both life and light in His gospel for the darkness of our world. It is the job of the church and of Christians to believe that gospel, cherish it, love it, proclaim it, and broadcast it. For the most part, the institutional church in the Middle Ages did not do this. The church of that day had not grasped the gospel message of light to speak into the darkness, and they failed to fully understand God's message of life in order to speak into the death that closed in from every direction. The light of the gospel was hidden, and darkness, as in the primordial days, covered the earth. The situation in the sixteenth century world could not have been more dire. And then an unknown Augustinian monk made the historical scene. Luther did not find the message of light and life by casting about in the wisdom and knowledge base of his day. He found that message of light and life by following ancient paths. Those ancient paths led him to timeless truth.

In the twenty-first century we are consumed with the present, with what's happening now, and with timely events. Every few minutes we check our news feeds to make sure we aren't missing anything. We used to say, "That's yesterday's news." We exchanged that for the expression, "That's so five minutes ago." What's next? "Sorry. You're a few seconds behind. Get with it."

We are consumed with timely messages, and a good portion of what we hear is not good news. We hear of increased security alerts because of on-line chatter about new methods terrorists are using to strike us. We are mired in political and economic turmoil because the new currency of debate is simply anger and rage. Companies used to build buildings from which to work. Now they build compounds.

I recently drove by Koch Industries in Wichita, Kansas, with a former executive. He told me how, at one time, a visitor could have driven right up to the front entrance and walked directly into the building. Now the corporate offices are surrounded by bunkers, and the entrances are choked off by gates and security houses.

Private security firms are thriving in this environment of the new normal. Governments regularly issue terror alerts, upgrading them frequently. Suicide bombers strike unsuspecting civilians attending a concert, eating at a restaurant, or walking down a street.

Much of the "timely" is bad news. We need a message of good news, but we will not find that message by looking to the current horizon. We must retrieve the timeless message.

Ultimately, the answer to intellectual, cultural, moral, economic, and spiritual darkness is the timeless message of the gospel and the timeless truth found in the Bible. A leader who stands only within a timely message is not a leader. One who stands only within the timely is part of the herd. Instead, a leader is one who looks to the timeless and time-tested. God's Word declares that it alone is eternal and abiding. All other words are passing, like the fading beauty of a flower and the wilting of the grass.

Luther faced a challenge, and he faced opposition. To speak to the challenge and to overcome the opposition, he looked for a sure and firm place to stand. He found it in the Word of God. He declared, "I'll trust in God's unchanging Word."

What did he find when he looked to the Bible? Luther concluded that the Bible is "a book of divine promises." He added, "God promises, offers, and gives us all His possessions and benefits in Christ." That's good news. All the possessions of God and all of His benefits—every possible and highest good—are in the gospel as revealed in the Word of God. In the Bible is a message of life and light. In the Bible is the answer to death and darkness. The Bible alone is the good news.

Luther found the Bible to be a nearly endless treasure trove of wisdom. For a season, he used Psalm 25:1 as a motto: "May integrity and uprightness preserve me." What would our days look like if we lived by that? How would our relationships change? What would our interactions with others look like? What if that motto governed all our business dealings? Biblical books, like Proverbs, overflow with wisdom for living. There is timeless truth and wisdom in the Word of God. A good leader knows that.

Luther also teaches us one more thing about the message. While it is a timeless message, it can be told in timely ways. The printing press was one of the technological innovations of the day that Luther employed. Woodcuts, another innovation, were used for creating an early version of political cartoons. An artist would carve into a level block of wood leaving grooves and gouges. The printer then applied ink to the raised parts on the woodblock, leaving the impression of the image behind. An example of an often-occurring woodcut in the 16th century was a two-panel image depicting Christ in the first panel. Typically, he would be among the poor and modestly dressed. The second panel would be entitled “Antichrist” and usually depict a bishop, cardinal, or the pope lavishly outfitted. Woodcuts could provide powerful messages through images. The proverbial picture is worth a thousand words.

Luther studied both of these innovations. He realized the power of this new media, and he used it to communicate the timeless message.

We should realize that most communication is battle communication. People are locked in a battle of ideas. False ideas were told with all the trappings of power in Luther's day. Might made right. But Luther never conceded an inch. He trusted in the power of the truth.

In the twenty-first century we are also in a battle of ideas. We live in an age where manipulation is the norm. The temptation is to shade the truth. Some have even asked, "Is truth dead?" No, it is alive and well. It is always timely and effective to simply tell the truth.

In addition to his understanding of media and negative communication, Luther also knew the value of the well-spoken word. He understood the power of drama, and in the pulpit and the classroom he not only proclaimed the truth, he proclaimed it persuasively and artfully. Luther's timeless message, well-told and empowered, changed the world. Actually, it turned the world upside down. In fact, his message was so timeless and so persuasive that we continue to listen to him 500 years later.

Luther also knew the power of a concise message. Although his writings fill close to two hundred volumes, he only wrote a few books, such as *The Bondage of the Will.* He primarily wrote what we would call pamphlets. These were called *Flugschriften* in German. They were eight—or sixteen-page booklets that could be written quickly, printed rapidly and cheaply, and easily transported and distributed. They allowed Luther to respond immediately to issues as they came up. Writing short pamphlets enabled Luther to keep up with his writing amid a busy schedule of teaching, preaching, and administrating. Luther was not the first person to employ the pamphlet as a tool for reaching people, but he came near to perfecting it with a great deal of efficiency and effectiveness.

Luther utilized the greatest technological advancements of his day, and he mastered the medium. Because of his deftness he could extend his influence. These *Flugschriften* meant that tens of thousands would be reading Luther and exposed to his ideas.

Just as Luther endeavored not to overtax readers, he endeavored not to overtax listeners. Luther once quipped, "When I have nothing left to say, I stop talking." He didn't keep circling the plane and wearying his listeners. He knew how to land the plane. Introductions need to hook. The body of the speech needs to convince, but finally you have to stick to the landing. That should be a cardinal rule taught in all speech classes. Say it, say it well, and, above all, know when to stop.

To tell timely truth is not leadership. That's simply reporting and identifying trends. Many can do that. To tell timeless truth in untimely ways is not leadership either. To do that is to squander opportunities. That's having a platform and blowing it.

Leaders tell timeless truth in timely ways. They know the power of the written and spoken word, and they know just the right package for each. When a timeless and truthful word is told well, it can change the world.

LEADERSHIP LESSON #2

Boldness and Confidence

Boldness and confidence come not from within, but from God.

Luther's most well-known piece of writing is a hymn. While "The Ninety-Five Theses" are the root of his fame, very few people have actually ever read them. But over the last five centuries, it's no exaggeration to say that millions of people have sung Luther's hymn, "A Mighty Fortress is Our God." It's an anthem, the battle-cry of the Reformation. "A Mighty Fortress Is Our God" is full of vivid lines and drama. One such line declares, "Did we in our own strength confide, our striving would be losing."

Luther understood and experienced conflict. One word used to describe Luther's early decades is the word *anfechtungen*, a German word that means struggles, deep and agonizing struggles. For the early decades of Luther's life many of those struggles were internal. Like Jacob wrestling with an angel, Luther wrestled with God. He didn't understand God. He had no idea how he could please God, yet he knew that his temporal life and his eternal life depended on it. He even entered the monastery in an attempt to somehow appease God, and he threw himself into his monastic duties.

On July 2, 1505, Luther was caught in a violent thunderstorm, which he took as an act of divine judgment against him personally. In the midst of thunder claps and lightning strikes, he vowed that if God would spare his life, he would enter the monastery. He did enter the monastery, even as a monk his struggle with God continued year after year. The sheer intensity and pace of it nearly killed him. Later in his life he would physically suffer for the abuse he had inflicted on his body during those years in the monastery.

His internal struggles came to a resolution only when he looked outside of himself. Luther liked to use a Latin word to describe himself as a sinner. He said that we naturally suffer from *incurvitas*, the self curved inward. Luther tried to overcome this sin by his own striving, but he failed.

The discovery that made the difference for Luther was that of "alien righteousness." This is not a religion from outer space! The righteousness that pleases a holy God comes from outside of us. It is alien to us. It is a righteousness that Christ, the perfect man and perfect God, can impute to us through His sacrificial death on the cross and our acceptance of His substitutionary death for us. This was the solution to Luther's internal struggles.

Later in life, Luther would have many external struggles and conflicts. Just naming them is exhausting. He struggled against the entire Roman Catholic Church—the largest institution of his day. He struggled against the Holy Roman Empire. And while, as historians say, it was not very holy, nor Roman, nor an empire, it was still formidable.

Martin Luther stood against popes, bishops, emperors, dukes. At the Diet of Worms in 1521, he stood before such a group of nobles and elites. They were decked out in their finery and the trappings of their office. Luther stood before them in his simple tunic with a rope for a belt. And he stood alone.

In 1525, when the peasants voiced their just complaints against the nobility, Luther stood with them—and at great personal risk and cost. Yet he also counseled them not to resort to violence and to be strategic as they made their case. The peasants did not heed his advice. When they turned to violence and tried to make their case as an angry marauding mob, Luther stood up and condemned them. He was in a no-man's-land, held in contempt by the nobles and viewed as a traitor by the peasants. His reputation still suffers to this day for the stand he took.

Luther had many friends who deserted him or betrayed him. They went after him, at times, with even greater ferocity than his enemies. Luther, it seems, was a man born to conflict, strife, and struggle.

There should be very little doubt that courage, boldness, and confidence are necessary for leadership. From the battlefield to the business meeting, timidity could cost you severely. Luther had boldness. It was not simply that he told timeless truths in a timely manner—he also told them boldly. He declared, "Here I stand. I can do no other."

The question is: Where did that boldness come from? He had training and a solid academic pedigree. He had earned his master's and his doctorate in jurisprudence and, after he entered the monastery, he earned yet another set of master's and doctoral degrees in theology and biblical studies.

Luther had a relentless work ethic, learned from watching his hard-working mother and father. His father managed a mine and, to help fund his son's education, he moonlighted by taking on a second mine. As long as Luther was living at home, he watched his father work two jobs. He watched his mom carry firewood on her back and labor to keep the Luther household functioning.

Luther carried his parents' drive and ambition with him when he left their home. He was a stellar student at every step of his academic journey. He kept a schedule of a furious pace. He was the kind of person who spent little time reflecting on past victories. Instead, he always asked what challenge would be next. He moved on to the next book to write, the next sermon to preach, the next issue to debate, the next battle to fight.

While he had top-tier training and personal fortitude, he also knew that if he placed confidence in his own strength, he would lose. He had confidence but not in himself.

Ultimately, Luther's boldness, courage, and confidence came from without, not from within. Luther could be confident because he had put his confidence in God. This was both a great inspiration to Luther and a great comfort to him as well. Knowing that God is our "Mighty Fortress" inspires us to enter the battle. And knowing that God is "a bulwark never failing" gives us comfort no matter what is happening. Late at night when the demons of doubt came, and they came often to Luther, he could rest in God, his "Mighty Fortress."

At the end of Luther's hymn, he can say, "the body they may kill." This is not because he's careless or capricious. It's because he knows he's in God's hands. He knows that God's eternal purposes will come to pass. He knows that God's Kingdom is forever and that God's truth abides.

General George Patton said that on the battlefield you need speed, simplicity, and boldness. Leaders need to be bold. Bold leaders need a place upon which to stand. Luther reminds us to look outside ourselves and to look to God.

LEADERSHIP LESSON #3

Perseverance

All leaders will face opposition, conflict, distortion, rejection, suffering, and loss— and know how to persevere through all of it.

As mentioned, Luther was no stranger to conflict or suffering. He suffered physically into his old age, and once he described himself as "an old man, decrepit, tired, sluggish, and cold." He was on his death bed several times before recovering and getting back in the game. Like an old car, the years and the miles, had taken their toll.

He also watched his family suffer. Luther and his wife Katie lost an infant son. They also watched their fourteen-year-old daughter, Magdalena, fall ill of a fever and die.

Her death devastated Luther. The plague hit Wittenberg on a few occasions. At one point, Frederick the Wise, the Elector of Saxony, ordered the University of Wittenberg closed and ordered the faculty and students to leave the city. Luther, who usually did what Frederick told him to do, disregarded the order. He turned his home into a makeshift hospital and cared for the sick. All of these occasions had the net effect of bringing suffering rather close to Luther. Again and again, suffering hit home for this giant from history. Our historical figures are not skimpy encyclopedia entries. They lived real, and oftentimes rather challenging, lives.

Another source of trials for Luther was the distortion of his teachings by opponents who published their own pamphlets in a smear campaign. They had their own woodcuts commissioned to portray Luther as the mouthpiece of Satan. He was depicted as the enemy of Germany.

When Pope Leo X issued the decree to excommunicate Luther in 1520, he called Luther a wild boar who was trampling the gospel of Christ underfoot. Luther was portrayed as an enemy of the gospel even though he was proclaiming it.The subject of rumors and gossip, he faced wave after wave of persecution. To complicate matters, Luther's followers had a tendency to take his teaching to extremes. They literally went wild in the city of Wittenberg by smashing stained glass windows and putting an axe to the organ. They toppled statues and removed artwork. They so wanted to rid the church of these Roman practices that they went to extremes. After Luther was condemned to death at Worms, he was "kidnapped" and taken to Wartburg Castle overlooking the town of Eisenach in Germany. He was actually taken by the friendly forces of Frederick the Wise and sent to Wartburg where he was hidden until things died down. Meanwhile, back in Wittenberg, his followers were so intent on expunging any trace of Roman

Catholicism in the city that they destroyed stained glass windows, statues, and paintings in the churches and chapels around the city. It became quite a dangerous situation. Luther left the safe confines of Wartburg to return to Wittenberg and put an end to the chaos.

Friends and foes alike made life difficult for Luther. Nevertheless, he persevered. This is not to say he was perfect. Luther had legs of iron, but he also had feet of clay. He could overreact and make rash judgments. His gift of having a way with words was often used poorly and improperly when he said vitriolic and hateful things. Despite his shortcomings, one thing Luther did not do was give up. He persevered.

We see this perseverance even in the events surrounding his death. He was called to come to the aid of his home city of Eisleben. A dispute about an inheritance embroiled some of the key families in that region, and the ripple effects threatened the church and city itself. It would not be a good thing for Luther's hometown to collapse. His enemies would have a field day with that, to be sure. It would also send tremors throughout Germany. Luther was tired. He longed for rest, but his presence was necessary, so he went.

The winter journey proved difficult. Luther fell ill along the way, but he continued the journey. When he got to Eisleben and heard the dispute, he was able to settle it. While he was there, he preached a number of times, but he was coming to the end of his earthly life. Luther died there in his home city on February 18, 1546. He had persevered until the very end.

We have come to think of suffering and hardship as the abnormal in our lives. For Luther, they were the normal. Even though he had many victories and celebrations, his life was difficult and full of sorrows and cares.

Leaders who are unprepared for distortion, rejection, suffering, and loss probably will not be able to endure in leadership roles.

Most leaders are involved in meaningful work, producing things of genuine benefit and promoting ideas that matter. Things of value and merit simply do not come easily. For leaders, very few days go off without hiccups, and very few journeys lack hardship and difficulty. Leaders don't assume otherwise.

Luther reminds us of two things as we think of his hardships. First, such things naturally attend leadership. Second, leaders must persevere through them.

One of those who followed Luther was his own wife Katie. After his death, she had severe difficulties. She faced economic challenges and she suffered physically. At one point during this extremely trying time, she wrote a letter to a friend saying, "I find myself clinging to Christ like a burr to a dress." She, too, learned the lesson of perseverance.

Another great leader of the twentieth century reminds us of this lesson. Winston Churchill's famous "Never, never, never give up" speech was able to steel a nation that was staring down the single greatest threat to their existence in the modern world. They persevered. The people of Britain would "never surrender."

Luther's life is a reminder of how essential the quality of perseverance is to leadership and to life.

LEADERSHIP LESSON #4

Potential of Children

Never underestimate the potential of children.

Luther seemed to have people coming at him from all directions all the time. The pulls and demands on his schedule were staggering. At Wittenberg he had two large churches for which he was responsible, the Castle Church and the city or state church, known as St. Mary's Church. He was de facto president of the University of Wittenberg, as well as its star faculty member. As the center of the Protestant Reformation, he was constantly writing. Yet every day he opened the doors of his home and invited in the children of Wittenberg as he taught them the catechism alongside his own children.

Luther would often take his eyes off the adults in the congregation, who stood during the service in those days, and focus squarely on the children. Luther knew that if he did not teach the gospel to children, then all his efforts to reform the church and culture would be for naught. If he didn't reach the next generation, reformation of the church would be in vain. Children did not put money in the coffers. They could not advance the mission through their positions and through their influence. They were not what we would call "strategic." Despite that, Luther never underestimated their potential and rarely did he pass up the opportunity to influence them.

Of course, leaders need to use their time wisely and invest in their lieutenants, clients, and supporters, but a leader who can take the time to speak to and influence a child can make an impact that will last for years and through generations. In a similar application, prudent leaders will invest time and attention in their younger employees, workforce, or direct reports. Young people need to learn from the leader's experience and his organizational knowledge base. The next generation will thrive and grow in the workplace with a leader's guidance. A leader's investment of time and teaching is a way to extend his or her legacy beyond one lifetime and into the generation to come.

I can vividly remember as a child when adults spoke to me on my level. They didn't pander. They stopped, even stooped down to look me in the eye and very clearly let me know that I was not a distraction from their real work. They gave me attention. Also, I remember senior stakeholders in places where I worked who helped me understand and taught me about the organization. Their impact was huge.

When I travel or speak at conferences, I love to meet folks of all ages, but I really enjoy meeting children. I shake their hands. I ask them what books they are reading. They tell me their names, the names of their pets, and their favorite subjects in school. Children potentially have seven or eight decades ahead of faithful and fruitful service. I want them to know that they matter, and I want to influence them.

Luther knew the children were crucial to the Reformation. He knew that what he was building was not just for the 1510s and 1520s. He knew that these were eternal truths for generations to come.

Leaders should not overlook children. They should not scorn or frown on them, either. Instead, leaders should recognize the value of children and take the time to stoop down and look them in the eye.

To say that leaders should never underestimate the potential of children is also to say that they should never underestimate their constituents who represent "the least of these." In fact, Jesus Himself knew the worth and importance of children. In the same way, He also recognized the value of women, despite the fact that they were overlooked and marginalized in His culture. Jesus spent far more time with the types of people who were deemed as less significant than with those who were considered important by the culture of the day. He didn't appraise people according to what they could do for Him. Instead, He approached people asking what He could do for them.

No doubt leaders need to be intentional with their time because all leaders have limited resources, and one of the most precious of those limited resources is time. But the key issue is how people are valued and calibrated. Leaders can miss out on opportunities by valuing time over people and by underestimating the potential of those they might too easily disregard or ignore.

Luther teaches leaders to stoop down, to look, and to pay attention. If you choose to follow Luther's example, you could be extending your influence for generations to come.

LEADERSHIP LESSON #5

Service

Leaders serve.

Luther always enjoyed a good paradox. One of his most popular books opens with one. The book is *On Christian Liberty*, written in the fall of 1520 at the very same time he was being excommunicated by the pope. The paradox is this: "The Christian is a completely free lord of all, subject to none. The Christian is a completely dutiful servant of all, subject to all."

Now this is a paradox, not a contradiction. Luther helps us understand more fully how these two maxims support each other. In short, he explains that because we are free, we are free to serve.

At one point in this book, Luther writes about self-discipline. He says that we should not "work on" ourselves for the sake of ourselves. Instead, "the purpose of putting the body in subjection is so that it can serve others more genuinely and freely." He adds, "Indeed, more to the point, each person lives only for others and not for himself or herself." We work and live for others. Freely. Willingly. Abundantly. These are all words Luther used to describe how we serve others.

Luther liked a woodcut that demonstrated this vividly. The woodcut consisted of two panels that contrasted two people. On the one side was a picture labeled "Christ." The other was labeled "Antichrist." On the one marked "Antichrist," the leaders are being attended to and even fawned over. People are kissing their rings, anointing their feet, fanning them with palms, and displaying solicitous expressions as if to say, "What can we get for you?" No one in that picture is standing taller than the leader.

The other panel has the leader on his knees. Everyone in the picture is higher than the leader. They are seated comfortably or standing around. The leader, Christ, is washing his disciples' feet. Christ is asking, "What can I do for you?" In one panel the leader is being served. In the other, the leader is serving. Luther sees such servant leadership as not only a time-tested reflection of the practices of Christ, but he also sees servant leadership as liberating and joy-inducing. Luther would say that to be a servant leader is both a duty and a delight. One incident, among many, in the life of Luther bears this out. The incident concerns Andreas Karlstadt, Luther's senior colleague at Wittenberg. He led the extreme reactions at Wittenberg that forced Luther out of hiding and caused him to return to the city. Luther and Karlstadt were in conflict over the next two years from 1521 to 1523. Then Karlstadt left to pastor at another city. The tensions between the two men grew even worse as they both wrote pamphlets against each other.

Luther deemed Karlstadt a dangerous radical. The two met at the Black Bear Inn in Jena, Germany. Their conversation did not go well. Luther ended it by tossing Karlstadt a guilder, worth about a day's wages, and telling him to keep on writing against him. It had devolved into a chilly relationship.

But their tensions took an unexpected turn during the Peasants' War when Karlstadt had to flee his home. The position he had taken put him in jeopardy, and there were threats on his life. With nowhere to go, Luther invited him into his home. Despite the four years of conflict and argument between the two men, Luther sheltered Karlstadt secretly in his home for eight weeks. Very few people knew what Luther had done for Karsltadt. When his enemy was in need, Luther served.

Legend has it that Katie took to hiding things she did not want Luther to give away. People often came to Luther's door with stories of their dire circumstances and requests for help from the good Dr. Martin Luther. After he discerned a genuine need, Luther would look around the house to find something of value that he could live without. The object would become a gift to the needy person, so if there was something precious or a family heirloom that Katie wanted to preserve, she would hide it, keeping it from the generous hands of her husband. Luther's judgment on some of these scores could be debated, but what the facts establish is this: Luther lived to serve others.

Luther could have easily exalted himself as a pope over this new movement he started. Many of his enemies accused him of starting the Reformation so he could do exactly that. Yet Luther never assumed any such position. This was not a case similar to Shakespeare's *Julius Caesar,* who refused the crown three times before "reluctantly" accepting it and revealing that he wanted the title all along. Luther did not ascend to a throne, nor did he want a crown. Luther was aware of the negative trappings of power.

Luther knew it was far better to serve. Leaders serve.

Serving requires humility. Among the very last words uttered by Luther are these: "We are beggars. This is true."

Humility requires gratitude. They often go hand in hand. Grateful people realize they need others and that others need them. They can set aside their own agendas to advance the agendas of those around them.

Dietrich Bonhoeffer, a Lutheran theologian who learned most of what he knew from Martin Luther's writing and influence, faced down Hitler and the Nazis. He was arrested and spent most of the war in prison. He was hanged at Flossenburg concentration camp on April 9, 1945, just weeks before the Allied Forces rolled in and liberated that camp. He was only thirty-nine years old.

Bonhoeffer endured air raids and the confines of his cell. He acutely faced the pain of separation from his parents, siblings, students, colleagues, and his fiancée. He persevered through all of the anxiety that whirled like a tornado around his life. During his tribulation he said, "How can we not do this if we are basically not grateful people?" When we realize that we are beggars—that all we have comes from, by, and through the mercy, goodness and kindness of God, we will be that kind of grateful person, that kind of humble person, that kind of servant.

Gratitude leads to humility. Humility leads to service.

The opposite is also true. Ingratitude is spawned from an attitude of independence, the false view that you need no one else. Ingratitude leads to independence, independence leads to arrogance and, arrogance leads to taking advantage of other people for your personal gain.

After his years of research and observation while poking around hundreds of companies, Jim Collins tells us that arrogance leads to something else: failure.

For some time Jim Collins has beat this drum about the necessity of humility. In his 2009 book, *How the Mighty Fall*, he documents how companies that have an ethos of arrogance are on the first step to an almost certain decline. Collins identifies the qualities of what he calls "Level 5 Leadership," the leadership that takes companies from "good to great." He distills the list down to two essential qualities: a dogged determination and an attitude of humility.

Peter Drucker's well-known maxim comes into play here: "Culture eats strategy for breakfast, lunch, and dinner." You can have the best strategies. You can have the best product, the most qualified team, the best industry standards in operation, the best marketing, and the best delivery systems. But a culture of arrogance or of "incurvitas," of being inward-focused and self-serving, will grind the whole thing to a halt.

Leo X, the pope during Luther's time, lacked humility. He never stopped to ask what he could learn from Martin Luther. He never thought for a minute that Luther was worth his time or that Luther might have something valuable to say. When Leo X first heard "The Ninety-Five Theses," he said, "The ramblings of a drunken German. He will think differently when he sobers up." Leo X's dismissive attitude cost him dearly. He entered the history books as having the greatest crisis in the Roman Catholic Church on his watch. Arrogance leads to failure.

How can we define this essential quality, humility? We start with what it's not. It's not passivity. It's not feigned modesty or low self-esteem. It's not, though it's often confused with, humiliation. John Dickson defines it in his book, *Humiltas*: "Humility is the noble choice to forgo your status, deploy your resources or use your influence for the good of others before yourself. " He adds, "More simply, you could say the humble person is marked by *a willingness to hold power in service of others*."

Luther both withheld his power and used his power in the service of others. Because of his courageous stand at the Diet of Worms in 1521, Luther spent most of his adult life as an outlaw. He had a death sentence on his head from 1521 until his death by natural causes in 1546. Luther willingly placed himself at great risk for what he believed was the good of his fellow Germans. He subjugated his personal desires to his ministry as a pastor. In actuality, Luther put the good of generations to come ahead of himself. As a humble man, Luther was a great man of nearly untold influence.

Conclusion

Leaders know that the most timely message is timeless truth, and they know how to tell it well.

Leaders must be bold and confident, and they must realize that the kind of boldness and confidence needed comes from God, not from within.

Leaders face all sorts of opposition and conflict, distortion, and even rejection—yet they persevere through it.

Leaders never underestimate the potential of children or of "the least among us."

Leaders serve.

Many more lessons could be added to this list of five. Martin Luther appeared on the historical scene during a time of a severe famine in leadership. There were plenty of problems that needed solving in the sixteenth century, but few people were trying to solve them. Leo X was only one of many leaders who missed the opportunity to influence, serve, and help.

Luther's leadership occurred largely within the church, but he was also a leader in the academy. Grounded and solid in the gospel message, he employed innovative and creative methods to communicate it. Entrepreneurial and bold, he was not afraid to take risks and deal with mistakes. My boss, the theologian R.C. Sproul, likes to say that while Luther stood firm, he did not stand still. He served as a pioneer from the posting of "The Ninety-Five Theses" on October 31, 1517, to his defense at the Diet of Worms on April 18, 1521. Luther fomented the Reformation and was at the very center of it. Then he spent fully twenty-five years, from 1521 until his death in 1546, working to establish the Protestant church in Germany and across Europe.

Luther was a reformer and scholar but, above all, he remains a leader worth following.

QUOTABLE LUTHER:

Luther on Life and Leadership

"When I have nothing more to say, I stop talking."

"The foolish account a matter to be indisputable for the sole reason that it has been espoused by the crowd."

"My father was a poor copper miner in his youth. Mother carried all the firewood home on her back. That was how we were brought up."

"To stand still on God's way means to go backwards, and to go forward means ever to begin anew."

*"God wants no lazy idlers,
but each should work hard and
faithfully, following his calling and
fulfilling his office, that God give him
blessing and cause him to thrive."*

*"Man is born to work as
the birds are born to fly."*

*"Only a humble man can
prefer another in honor."*

*"What a great service it is to yield
honor to someone else!"*

*"The clear and distinct norm
of every rulership is diligence."*

*"The world is filled
with daily wonders."*

"We should not use force
to stand against the powers that be,
but we should only stand for the truth."

"Here I stand. I can do no other.
God help me."

"Be refreshing.
Be clear. Be brief."

"Beware of the man of one book."

"Never judge anyone before
the other side is heard."

"Don't believe everything you hear.
Don't speak everything you know.
Don't do everything you can."

"The time for silence has passed,
and the time for action has come ."

"I enter the fray after careful reflection."

"Our Lord God made the best gifts
the most common ... But we don't
acknowledge such everyday gifts."

"Don't put off till tomorrow!
By delay Hannibal lost Rome.
By delay Esau forfeited his birthright."

LIGONIER MINISTRIES

Renew your Mind.

Dr. Stephen Nichols also serves as the Chief Academic Officer of Ligonier Ministries. Ligonier Ministries is an international Christian discipleship organization founded by theologian Dr. R.C. Sproul in 1971 to equip Christians to articulate what they believe, why they believe it, how to live it, and how to share it. Proclaiming God's holiness is central to Ligonier's purpose. Ligonier produces Renewing Your Mind radio broadcasts, the Reformation Study Bible, Tabletalk magazine, books through the Reformation Trust Publishing division, and various teaching series. It also offers academic degrees through Reformation Bible College. In addition, Ligonier hosts national and regional conferences, offers an online learning community through Ligonier Connect, streams twenty-four-hour Christian internet radio through RefNet, and makes available more than 8,000 unique resources online at Ligonier.org.

Reformation Bible College

Dr. Nichols is the President of Reformation Bible College. Founded by Dr. R.C. Sproul in 2011, Reformation Bible College is located in Sanford, FL and offers undergraduate degrees in biblical and theological studies, and sacred music. RBC strives to give students a thorough knowledge of the Scriptures and Christian Reformed doctrine, gained through the core curriculum which includes courses in Bible, systematic theology, the great works of philosophy, literature, and music; as well as courses in apologetics, church history, and languages. RBC purposes to advance the Kingdom of God by educating the next generation for a new Reformation. Find out more at ReformationBibleCollege.org.

NOTES

NOTES

NOTES

NOTES

NOTES

NOTES

NOTES

NOTES

NOTES

NOTES

NOTES